THE STORY OF GAUTAMA BUDDHA

The Prince Who Ran Away

by ANNE ROCKWELL

illustrated by FAHIMEH AMIRI

ALFRED A. KNOPF
New York

More than two thousand years ago, there lived a rich rajah and a beautiful queen.

Beyond their palace rose the high, snowcapped Himalayan mountains, whose melting snow sent fresh water to the plains below. Forests of sweet mango trees were filled with bright-colored singing birds. The fields were full of stalks of rice, so there was plenty of food for all the people the rajah ruled. The rajah and queen had everything in the world—except a child. With all their blessings, they could not be happy, for they wanted a child very badly.

One night the queen had a strange dream. An elephant white as snow, its skin glistening like ice, with eyes like gold and tusks that shone like silver, came down from the highest mountain. It held a lotus blossom in its trunk and ran toward the queen, trumpeting loudly. She was frightened, but the beautiful elephant suddenly stopped running and didn't trample her.

When she woke the next morning, the queen commanded that the holiest man in the kingdom be summoned from his cave in the mountain to explain the meaning of her dream, for she was sure it was an important one.

The holy man said the dream meant the queen would soon have a son who would be a great leader. The rajah and queen were overjoyed.

When the time came near for the baby to be born, the queen left the palace to go to her mother and father's home to give birth, as was the custom. But she didn't get far. While she and her handmaidens were passing through a forest filled with flowering trees, the little prince was born.

His hair was black and shining as the night, and his skin was burnished dark gold like the morning sun. As soon as he was born, a pair of elephants came and showered the baby with warm, then cool water from their trunks. Fragrant flowers fell from the trees and covered him. His baby cries were as melodious as the singing birds that surrounded him. His name was Siddhartha Gautama.

Although the rajah was overjoyed at the sight of his little son, he felt a great sadness, too. For the baby's mother died after only seven days. The rajah's sister and many nursemaids took care of the newborn prince, and he called the wise Brahmans in his kingdom to come and tell the baby's fortune.

When the wisest of them examined the baby, he noticed a pattern of perfect little wheels on the soles of his tiny feet.

"These represent the wheel of life, from which none of us can escape," the Brahman said. "These wheels mean there is a great destiny awaiting your son."

"The holy man of the mountain also said that," said the rajah. "But please tell me exactly what my son's destiny will be."

"All I can tell you is that if Prince Siddhartha lives in a palace, he will be the greatest and most powerful rajah in the world," the Brahman said. "But if he lives outside the palace, he will be a beggar. All the suffering he sees in the world will make him suffer, and he will be too compassionate to bear it."

When the rajah heard this, he vowed that Prince Siddhartha would never see suffering, for he would never allow his son to go outside the walls surrounding the palace.

The rajah built three new palaces, one for winter, one for spring, and one for the monsoon time, when it rained for months without stopping. All the palaces were filled with games and sweet perfume. There were storytellers, musicians, and dancers so the prince could never be bored. Every day, ice was brought down from the mountains and mixed with fruit juice to make rare and tasty sherbets for the prince.

The rajah built three pools that gardeners filled with beautiful lotus flowers for the boy to look at. Teachers came, and soon the prince knew all the languages of India and could read the picture writing of faraway China. He was never lonely, for his cousin Ananda became his playmate and best friend. He also had a pet parrot to talk with. A servant always walked beside him carrying a wide white umbrella so that Prince Siddhartha would never suffer from hot sun, or cold rain, or dry dust that might make him sneeze.

No person or creature who was old, sick, or suffering in any way could stay within the walls of the palace. Gardeners worked all night while the prince was sleeping so he wouldn't see them remove wilted flowers and leaves, pick up grasshoppers and other insects that had sung their song and died, or dispose of broken birds' eggs that had fallen from nests in the trees.

Prince Siddhartha's father gave him a horse and chariot and assigned a good man named Channa to be his driver. The prince and Channa rode around the vast palace gardens, which were as large as a city, but the gates leading out of the palace could never be opened for them.

The prince begged his father to let him go outside. Finally, the rajah had to say yes, for he had built a magnificent park, filled with places for every kind of sport known in the world. To reach it, Prince Siddhartha had to pass through the city.

The rajah was extremely careful. He had all the houses in the city painted bright and new. Any dying plants were replaced with healthy ones. All the people in the city were given new clothes and plenty to eat. The rajah ordered them to hide all their old and sick people inside. All the young, healthy, good-looking people and their children were to smile and be happy while Prince Siddhartha drove through the streets.

But on the road the prince suddenly saw someone walking with a bent spine and a cane. He had straggly white hair.

"Why is that man's hair so thin and strangely colored? Why doesn't he stand up and walk straight and tall?" the prince asked Channa.

"He's very old and lame," the charioteer replied. "As we all will be someday."

Prince Siddhartha looked at the old man's white hair and bent spine with horror. "Will you be old someday? Will I change like that? Will my father? Will Ananda?" he asked Channa.

"Yes. Each one of us will grow old, my lord, even your horse," the charioteer replied.

They went on a little farther and saw someone writhing on the ground with sickness and terrible pain. They passed a funeral procession and saw mourners sobbing, wailing, and smearing their faces with dirt.

So in one day Prince Siddhartha learned of old age, sickness, and death. Just as the wisest Brahman had said he would, he felt compassion. He was filled with sadness for all the people who suffered so.

"Is there no way to avoid old age, sickness, and death?" he asked Channa.

"No," said the charioteer. "We'll all die, but even death doesn't end our suffering. The wheel of life goes on turning, and we are all trapped on it. Each of us will be reborn in some form, whether human or animal, again and again, except for those who attain nirvana—who can see the truth in all things. Only they don't have to go on living, suffering, dying, and being born for more of the same."

Then Prince Siddhartha saw a beggar who was also a holy man, and he saw peace in the man's eyes. He thought of what Channa had told him and all he had seen that day. He wondered if there wasn't some way to end suffering. But he didn't tell anyone what he was thinking.

Mara, the Evil One, knew without being told what the prince was thinking. He saw what great compassion Prince Siddhartha felt for the suffering of others, and he was alarmed. For Mara was so evil that there was nothing he enjoyed more than the sight of someone in pain. He made up his mind to do everything possible to keep the prince from finding a way to end suffering.

Prince Siddhartha grew sadder and sadder as his compassion for everything in the world grew deeper and deeper. When the rajah saw how his son was often sad and thoughtful in spite of all the riches he had, he decided the young man must be lonely and that he should get married. A wife would surely make him happy.

The smartest, richest, and most beautiful young women in all the land were invited to come to the palace and meet the handsome prince. Each one was given a precious jewel by Prince Siddhartha, but he didn't choose one of them to marry. His father was very disappointed.

But then a princess arrived late, after all the other young women had gone. There were no jewels left to give her, but Prince Siddhartha knew immediately she was the one he wanted to marry. He took off the sparkling jewels he wore and gave them to this princess, whose name was Yasodhara.

After he was married to the beautiful and intelligent Yasodhara, Prince Siddhartha was so happy he forgot, for the moment, that he had seen suffering and felt such painful compassion. Instead he remembered some of his happier past lives and knew that Yasodhara had been his wife in those lives, too. He recalled one particularly happy life when he'd been a tiger roaming the green forest and Yasodhara had been his mate. He was overjoyed to have found her again.

One evening, the rajah gave a party, as he often did. Hundreds of dancing girls with tinkling golden bells on their wrists and ankles twirled their graceful arms and spun round and round to the music late into the night. But after the dancing had stopped and everyone had gone to bed, Prince Siddhartha roamed the halls of the palace, restless and unable to sleep.

When he came to the great hall, he saw the hundreds of dancing girls sprawled sweaty and exhausted on the floor. Some of them tossed and moaned in pain, rubbing legs and backs that were sore from so much dancing; he saw their bloody and blistered feet. Again Prince Siddhartha saw suffering and felt immense pity and compassion.

He decided he had to leave his father's palace and go out into the world to find a way to end suffering.

It was a painful decision, for Yasodhara had recently given birth to a baby boy. But in spite of this, Prince Siddhartha ordered Channa to fetch his horse and chariot. He could not bear to stay in the palace and was determined to leave while his father slept.

"My lord, surely you know that the rajah will not allow this," Channa said.

"That is why I must go while he is sleeping," the prince said.

"But why go, my lord? Everything anyone could ever want is here."

"I must go out into the world to find a way to end suffering," the prince said. "Now get my horse—and quickly!"

And Channa did as the prince commanded.

Prince Siddhartha couldn't bear to say good-bye to his wife and baby son. He loved them very much. He knew that if Yasodhara pleaded with him to stay, as he was sure she would, he could never leave her. When he looked at his beautiful sleeping wife and son, the prince experienced yet another kind of suffering—that of not being able to be with those he loved.

It was then he realized that love, too, could cause suffering, just as old age, illness, and death did.

"Fool! You could be a great and rich rajah—ruler of all the world!" Mara hissed as Channa took the reins of the horse.

But Prince Siddhartha kept his eyes steadily ahead and paid no attention to the Evil One.

By some miracle, the great gates opened without making a sound to awaken the rajah. The horse's hooves and the wheels of the chariot were silent, too, as Prince Siddhartha rode out into the moonlight. Wherever the chariot's wheels rolled, a path of flowers instantly bloomed. The chariot rolled faster and faster and Mara could not keep up with it.

Soon they came to a forest.

"I must say good-bye to you here, my friend," said the prince to Channa.

The man wept. The horse, too, cried human tears as it knelt to kiss the prince's feet.

The prince took off his princely clothes and jewels and walked into the forest, where he met a hunter. He asked the man to give him his ragged yellow leather robe, and the hunter did. Then Prince Siddhartha took his sword and chopped off his long hair, black and shining as the night, and threw it and the sword into the river. A beggar's bowl appeared before him. He was no longer Prince Siddhartha. Now he was simply Gautama, a common beggar, just as the wisest Brahman had predicted he would be.

When this happened, Mara was more afraid than ever that Gautama would succeed in discovering a way for people to end their suffering. If this happened, there would be no fun left for him, for the Evil One delighted in watching people suffer.

"Listen to me! Go back to your father's palace! Didn't I tell you you would soon be the greatest and richest rajah ever known—the most powerful in all the world?" Mara hissed once more. But again Gautama paid no attention to him.

Gautama went to a cave in the mountains where a holy man lived. Five other young men had come there to learn from him. The holy man told them they must starve themselves into suffering and pain, for that was the only way to truth.

Gautama did as the holy man told him. He sat until his yellow robe grew filthy and rotted. His bones grew stiff and ached, and he became so thin he was nothing more than a skeleton. His golden skin turned dull and dusty brown. His eyes sank deep into the hollows of his skull, although they still shone from the blackness like bright stars. But he did not learn truth or the right way to find it, although he certainly learned pain and suffering.

Now Gautama knew that the way to truth was not through too much pleasure, which he had learned in his father's palace, nor through too much pain. He was sure there was another way—a middle way between pleasure and pain.

A girl who lived in a nearby village came and fed the starving beggar some sweet rice pudding she had made with rich cream. Flesh covered his bones again, and his golden skin shone with health. He stood up and walked away while the other five young men mocked him.

"Look at Gautama!" they cried. "See how he is afraid to suffer bravely as we do. Ha! He doesn't have the courage to be a holy man!"

But Gautama just went on his way, carrying his beggar's bowl, begging for the food he needed wherever he went.

Gautama walked until he came to an enormous spreading fig tree—the great Bo Tree. He sat down under its branches, crossed his legs in front of him, placed his hands on his thighs, lowered his eyelids, and began to concentrate.

He concentrated on his life in the palace, all he had known before in his many lives, all he had never known. As he did, he saw how everything that has a beginning must also have an end. He saw how everything has its own dharma, or truth, and that the dharma of everything in the universe is change. As he concentrated, Gautama began to understand the meaning of all things, and this understanding brought him peace. He no longer felt suffering; his knowledge was so great. He smiled. He had discovered the truth he had been seeking.

When Mara saw Gautama sitting so peacefully under the great Bo Tree, he was very, very angry. He sent hideous demons to frighten Gautama away.

The demons leaped at him and screamed and made terrifying faces, but Gautama ignored them. They threw rocks at him, but all the rocks turned to soft flowers as soon as they struck him.

Finally, Gautama placed his palm calmly but firmly on the earth, and it opened. All Mara's ugly demons fell down into the dark crack in the earth and vanished.

Next Mara sent all his beautiful daughters to tempt Gautama to come away with them, but the peaceful beggar paid no attention to them.

Then Mara sent a terrible thunderstorm. Rain and hail pelted down through the thick green leaves of the great Bo Tree, but the king of the cobras came and coiled around Gautama as he sat. The snake's wide, flat head curved over him, protecting the poor beggar from the rain, just as the wide white umbrella in his father's gardens had once done.

At this, Mara gave up.

After seven weeks of sitting under the Bo Tree, Gautama found enlightenment, the light that shows the truth in all things, and he found nirvana, the peace that triumphs over suffering. He understood dharma, the law governing all things. Most important of all, Gautama had found this knowledge inside his own mind, nowhere else.

He knew there would always be old age, sickness, and death. He also knew nothing could change this, for all things that have a beginning must have an end. But Gautama had found a way to stop suffering through a deep concentration that led to peace. His compassion for other people made him want to share this knowledge with anyone who wanted to learn what he could teach.

He stood up from his place beneath the Bo Tree and began to walk. As he did, a bright light shone from within him and glowed around him. He was no longer simply Gautama, a common beggar. He was the Buddha, which means the Enlightened One.

Gautama Buddha traveled east. Wherever he went, he spoke gently and acted with kindness. Whenever he came to a village, he would sit down under the largest tree growing there, draw a circle in the dust, and wait patiently for whoever wished to hear him. Then he would begin to speak quietly and thoughtfully to those who came to learn. And there were many, including his old playmate, Ananda. People began to call him "The Learned One."

As the years went by, the Buddha taught thousands his way to the end of suffering. Then his students wandered throughout the world—begging as the Buddha did, wearing yellow robes as he did—to teach others what they had learned. Even the five young men who had mocked him when he chose the Middle Way came to listen and learn from him. Even the son he had left behind in the palace became one of the Buddha's many followers.

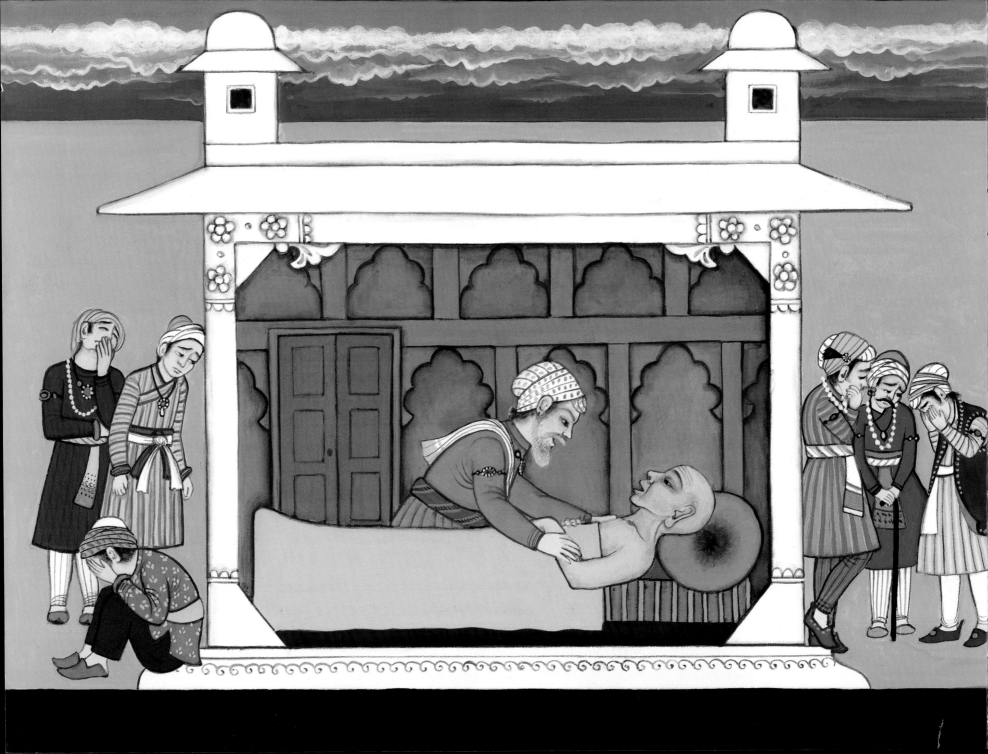

When he was eighty years old, the Buddha knew the time had come for him to die, for his dharma had been revealed to him.

That night, he ate some supper a poor man left out in his beggar's bowl. Either a poisonous mushroom from the forest was in the bowl or the food was rotten. Whatever the cause, the Buddha became very sick.

Ananda nursed him tenderly but saw it was no use. In spite of all his efforts, his beloved cousin and teacher, the frail and elderly Buddha, was going to die.

"Do not die," Ananda begged. "For if you leave us, who will be our teacher? Who will show us the way to nirvana and the enlightenment that conquers all suffering?"

The Buddha smiled. "Don't be sad when I die, my friend. Remember—all things that have a beginning must have an end. And haven't I taught you that the only way to nirvana lies within you, that you must find it for yourself?"

Ananda nodded.

"Keep the light that glows within you burning, for it alone will lead you to truth," the Buddha said. Then, still smiling, he closed his eyes for the last time and died.

His dharma was complete. His work was done. Never again would Gautama Buddha have to turn on the endless wheel of life, which Channa the charioteer had told him of so long ago when he was still only Prince Siddhartha, the pampered prisoner of his father's palace.

Author's Note Buddhism is one of the world's five major living religions. It is older than Christianity or Islam but younger than Judaism or Hinduism, from which it originated.

Gautama Buddha was a real person. He was, as this story tells, born to a rajah and his wife in the sixth century B.C. in what is today the country of Nepal, about a hundred miles from the modern Indian city of Varanasi. He lived to be very old. Gautama Buddha did tell stories of his early life in his father's palace to his followers, but the stories have probably been embellished over the past 2,500 years with far older legends, some borrowed from the vast and fantastic Hindu storytelling tradition into which Siddhartha Gautama was born.

I have chosen just a few incidents in the life of the Buddha—those I believe children will best understand and enjoy. I hope that readers will continue to discover more about him in other books.

The teachings of the Buddha spread during his lifetime, and after his death, far into the rest of the Asian world. Today, most of the people living in Asia are Buddhists. The teachings of the Buddha are undogmatic, thoughtful, and flexible. Each person may discover the truth in himself or herself by using the profound and intuitive guidelines the Buddha taught his followers.

For Nigel and Nancy—A.R.
For Ava—F.A.

THIS IS A BORZOI BOOK PUBLISHED BY ALFRED A. KNOPF

Text copyright © 2001 by Anne Rockwell. Illustrations copyright © 2001 by Fahimeh Amiri.
All rights reserved under International and Pan-American Copyright Conventions. Published in the United States of America by Alfred A. Knopf, a division of Random House, Inc., New York, and simultaneously in Canada by Random House of Canada Limited, Toronto. Distributed by Random House, Inc., New York. KNOPF, BORZOI BOOKS, and the colophon are registered trademarks of Random House, Inc.

www.randomhouse.com/kids
Library of Congress Cataloging-in-Publication Data
Rockwell, Anne.
The prince who ran away : the story of Gautama Buddha / by Anne Rockwell ; illustrated by Fahimeh Amiri.
p.   cm.
1. Gautama Buddha — Juvenile literature. [1. Buddha.] I. Amiri, Fahimeh, ill. II. Title.
BQ892 .R63 2001
294.3'63—dc21
00-067140
ISBN 0-679-89188-9 (trade)
ISBN 0-679-99188-3 (lib. bdg.)
Printed in the United States of America   November 2001   10 9 8 7 6 5 4 3 2 1   *First Edition*